CHRISTIANS?

CHRISTIANS?:

Common Decency

Translated by C. R. Mancari

Celestial Literary Group

Christians?: Common Decency

The contents of this book are not meant to take the place of qualified medical professionals or therapists. There is no expressed or implied guarantee regarding the effects of the suggestions given or the liability taken.

"And thou shalt love the Lord thy God with all thy heart, and with all thy soul, and with all thy mind, and with all thy strength: this is the first commandment. And the second is like, namely, this, Thou shalt love thy neighbor as thyself. There is none other commandment greater than these" (Mark 12: 30-31).

CONTENTS

PREFACE

This work came about because of the state of our country (USA); it is not from wars, invasions, or the threat of nuclear power. There is a much graver state than any nuclear power could cause. Yes, losing our lives is grave, but losing our souls is an eternal nuclear blast.

There is a lack of the very basics of our God-given nature, common decency. The Oval Office is no longer a place of common decency. The room that, at one time, was considered a place of honor has endured words of crude and bombastic rhetoric. The media news networks multiply the garbage by reporting it daily. Our souls are always under attack by the lack of leadership and the hypocritical silence of those who call themselves Christians.

I have spent ninety-three years on this earth, in this country, but never have I had to listen to and watch our beloved country being tarnished by tyrannical fools and those who would blindly support and emulate the worst among themselves. Jesus Christ was a savior in His time. Is there none in ours? Will common decency be restored? Like peace, it can be accomplished only if we are willing to rise to the occasion and stop the bloody massacre of common decency.

The intent of this work is for you, who lack the knowledge of your inherent nature of common decency, and therefore believe you have the free rein to mistreat your fellow human beings. Not so. It will bite you in the butt when you least expect it. So read, learn something about yourself, and be open to change for the sake of a Nation where Christianity is on life support.

Included are reviews of the Spiritual Center and the Christ Consciousness Meditation. It is hoped that these may help reveal your innate courage to rise and become the savior so desperately needed. The author acknowledges the necessity for law and order. However, it is not the law that is on trial here but the administering of the law and the injustice of the handling of fellow human beings.

The Bible scripture verses quoted are from The Holy Bible, King James Version, London: Syndics of Cambridge University Press, Bentley House, American Branch, New York, New York, printed in Great Britain.

ACKNOWLEDGMENTS

I am grateful for the Christians who are willing to express their non-compliance with the indecency on display at the highest levels. These are the brave, pure souls who are a testimony to the little common decency that remains.

I appreciate the help that Mary Carpenter so graciously offers. She reviewed and edited the manuscript.

I am thankful for the gift of the Christ Consciousness Meditation revelation and for all of you who it has helped. The Christian journey would be most difficult without it.

1

WHO IS
A
CHRISTIAN?
Bullyism

Christians are individuals who follow the teachings of Jesus Christ. Christian is a word much like the word love. So often used, it is open to a variety of interpretations *and* misinterpretations. Jesus did not teach hate, divisiveness, and name-calling. Jesus would never follow such an individual for *any* reason.

You cannot call yourself a Christian and then set aside Christian values for the convenience of getting something. Christian common decency does not work that way. Being a Christian is 24/7, no time off for bad behavior. So, why are there Christians hiding behind a bully? Why would Christians support a bully for *any* reason?

Do you *really* believe that Jesus Christ would trade His beliefs for any reason? Do you *really* believe that Jesus Christ could set aside His beliefs for a pay-off of any kind? Do you *really* believe that Jesus Christ would follow anyone who displayed anti-Christian acts? Do you *really* believe that Jesus Christ would support anyone who intentionally hurts another? Do you *really* believe that Jesus

Christ would sanction an individual who calls himself a Christian and is willing to set aside his Christian common decency to get something?

Understand that your religious beliefs are now what you are willing to support? You cannot play games with what you call religious beliefs. Yours are now founded not by Jesus Christ, but because you support the actions of a bully – you have been baptized into Bullyism. Not by water, not by fire, and not by spirit but by Bullyism (my word).

You cannot pretend to be a Christian when your silence demonstrates otherwise. Your absence of dissent is noticeable. A Christian sense of common decency is regrettably lacking.

If you are one of those who attend bullish rallies and is pumped up with hateful rhetoric, come back to the Christ of your Christian values. Stand out and stand up for those less fortunate. Realize that yours is not a religious belief founded on the persecution of your fellow human beings. Common decency is expected to avoid negative consequences. There *are* consequences.

2

CONSEQUENCES
Self-Inflicted

Christianity requires common decency. Individuals' lack of common decency has negative consequences. Consequences, positive or negative, result from individuals' behavior. Everything individuals do bears consequences. Subtle or obvious, consequences are inherent in every thought, word, and deed.

Consequences are not punishment. They are due process. Consequences are self-inflicted and result when operating within a set of rules, regulations, and laws. As a Christian, do not confuse forgiveness with consequences. Forgiveness does not exclude consequences. Scripture teaches forgiveness. Being forgiven does not excuse bad behavior from bearing consequences.

The common decency rules and laws of a society cause consequences when they are ignored or willfully broken. You may believe there are exceptions to the rule. However, consequences have a way of catching up when least expected.

Natural compliance with the laws of the universe results in decisions made from a place of responsibility for yourself and others. Common decency is a responsibility expected of a practicing Christian. In this life, upon this earth plane, the responsibilities may be endless, and the greater the number of responsibilities that are accepted, the more an individual may become attached to the importance of the responsibilities.

Some Individuals strive for more and more responsibilities to prove to others *and* themselves how important they are. On this earth plane, responsibilities are all about who and what you are as an identity. It may become an ego trip to a large extent.

In reality, there is always only one primary responsibility: common decency. If you fail at that, your self-imposed importance is a bloated proportion of hot air. Whatever services (responsibilities) are performed, all should be performed conscientiously with common decency. It may be easy to be fooled by the expectations that responsibilities may appear to present moment to moment. To forget that responsibilities carry consequences is playing a gigantic joke on you!

Christian is not an identity that you may acquire by waving a Bible around. It is a life lived from the awareness of the likeness and image of a loving and compassionate God. What price are *you* willing to pay to acquire, with greed, all that this world has to offer? What would *you* give in exchange for *your* soul?

"For what is a man profited, if he shall gain the whole world, and lose his own soul? Or what shall a man give in exchange for his soul?" (Matt: 16: 26).

3

TRAITS
Distinguishable Characteristics

So, what are the distinguishable characteristics of individuals who are hell-bent on destroying everything and everyone around them? There are many. Here are a few.

3. GREED

Greed is desire steeped in selfishness. Greed embodies willfulness, lack of trust, and lack of responsibility. It seeks to define individuals and the things of this world as "my, mine."

Greed leads individuals to be willing to trade the temporary for the permanent. Who would trade the kingdom of heaven for the kingdom of this world? *"And the world passeth away, and the lust thereof: but he that doeth the will of God abideth for ever"* (I John 2:17).

Scripture reveals greed as man's ignorance of his true nature. Jesus addresses greed in the parable of the rich man who would hoard his fruits by building greater barns. *"But God said unto him, Thou fool, this night thy soul shall be required of thee: then whose shall those things be, which thou hast provided?"* (Luke 12: 20).

This earth plane of opposites is immersed in human-made controls, rules, and laws that testify to the systemic greed that spreads its tentacles throughout human-kind's existence. A materialistic individual's underpinnings rest on a large dosage of greed. The goal is to ignore Christian core values to fulfill their desires by any means, regardless of the effect it may have on others' lives. *"He that is greedy of gain troubleth his own house; but he that hateth gifts shall live"* (Proverbs 15: 27).

The Individual who believes they must have all they desire, regardless of how it may affect others, is heading toward self-destruction. Desires may be fulfilled, but not at the expense of the welfare of others. What or who has caused anyone to ignore their innate nature of common decency? It is not their innate nature to be cruel to others. Yours is a kind, loving nature that is born of a God that is good. *"The Spirit itself beareth witness with our spirit, that we are the children of God"* (Romans 8: 16).

The power is in your God nature to overcome greed. *"For all that is in the world, the lust of flesh, and the lust of the eyes, and the pride of life is not of the Father but is of the world"* (I John 2: 16).

The God of your being meets your need, not greed. Greed is not in God's nature. Have you forgotten that the world of greed is not your world? *"They are not of the world, even as I am not of the world"* (John17: 16).

~ ~

2. EMOTIONAL ADDICTION

Emotional addiction is the constant feeding of a conditioned, preconceived, and deceptive emotional need. Addiction is not only a drug habit. Many possible emotional addictions may be every bit as strong as any drug.

An emotional addiction may be as debilitating and enslaving as drug addiction. It takes hold of an individual's time and energy. One of the strongest emotional addictions is the need to feel important. This need may stem from the early years of wanting to be noticed, from a lack of attention, or from the feeling of never quite measuring up.

Regardless of the ingrained conditioned cause, perpetually seeking ways to feed the addictive emotional need continues when left unchecked. What an incredible feeling of importance to believe that so many want your time and attention. The more you are in demand, the more valuable you feel. Oh, how important you are! Sure.

Feeding the emotional need for approval is a constant reminder of just how important you are. Yeah! Keeping the addictive emotional feeling of importance well-fed, the addiction itself becomes the priority. *"All the labour of man is for his mouth, and yet the appetite is not filled"* (Ecclesiastes 6: 7).

An emotional addiction may have such a stranglehold on an individual that the individual may often be swept along until the individual is drowning in commitments, projects, and appointments. It is the addiction that is directing the course of action on a path of self-destruction. *"In all thy ways acknowledge him, and he shall direct thy paths"* (Proverb 3: 6).

The addiction to feeling important is subtle and often goes unnoticed because of its deceptive nature. The addiction may be mistaken for genuine self-protection. An individual may want to believe others are being served when, in reality, the individual is serving the emotional addiction. That is the greatest deception ever perpetrated on an individual. *"The way of a fool is right in his own eyes: but he that hearkeneth unto counsel is wise"* (Proverbs 12: 15).

To pretend that others are being well served while seeking time and attention is a colossal joke being played on the individual— by the individual. *"What profit hath a man of*

all his labour which he taketh under the sun?"
(Ecclesiastes: 1: 3).

The emotional need of importance has no reality. It cannot be sustained, and rises and falls in a mental state of consciousness. It must continuously be fed anew. An individual cannot hold on to a feeling of importance because, in reality, it does not exist.

Compassionate service is a natural outpouring of a loving nature. However, all require a balance. No matter how the addiction to importance was created, an individual does have the power to overcome it. But, like any addiction, the individual is the one feeding it. And the individual is the one who must starve it.

~~

3. APPROVAL

Approval is the desire for a positive opinion or response from others. It is closely related to praise in that it seeks constant credit for every action. Seeking approval for the work that is done is the result of deep-seated cultural conditioning. Early in life, individuals may quickly have learned from family and friends what they would like or dislike about their behavior. They may have strived to meet others' standards and expectations. When they did not meet the standards and expectations, they quickly learned what disapproval felt like. Not a good feeling. Consequently, they did their best to avoid disapproval. In doing so, they inadvertently sought approval.

There is no harm in receiving approval. It is the seeking of approval and the fear of disapproval that cause the difficulty. Seeking the positive and fearing the negative are counterproductive in life. The gifts that individuals have received and are asked to share are severely limited in the shadow of fear. What can anyone do well, if it is at the mercy of seeking a stamp of approval and avoiding the fear of disapproval?

Whatever gifts individuals have to express on their life's journey are not subject to this world's approval or disapproval. If Jesus Christ sought approval and feared disapproval, He would not have continued past His first sermon. Jesus could never have fulfilled His mission on this earth if He sought the approval of those who heard His message. Jesus had reason to fear others' opinions, but He did not. Jesus knew who He was. He knew His mission, and He knew that the harm they sought to do to Him would be done to them.

Jesus' message did not need validation from anyone. Disapproval of His message did not affect its truth. Jesus did not labor in vain. He did not seek approval or fear disapproval. *"EXCEPT the LORD build the house, they labour in vain that build it . . ."* (Psalm 127: 1).

On a life's journey, there may be approval *and* disapproval. Certainly, accept approval with gratitude and avoid living in a selfish warp zone out of fear of disapproval. *"Fear thou not; for I am with thee; be not dismayed; for I am thy God: I will strengthen thee yea, I will help thee; yea I will uphold thee with the right hand of my righteousness"* (Isaiah 41: 10).

It is an individual's responsibility to do the work that is given, without needing to seek approval. *Are ye so foolish? Having begun in the Spirit, are ye now made perfect by the flesh?"* (Galatians 3: 3).

Red Flags that Signal a Need for Approval:

3.   Waiting for a response from your work

B. Living in fear of what you could lose.

C. Leading with your head, not your compassionate nature.

D. Modifying your work to gain approval.

E. Concerned about how others may judge your work.

F. Being relieved when others approve of you.

G. Weighing the possible cost of your position in life.

The best tool in a Christian's arsenal of overcoming the need for constant approval is to realize that the journey is one of love, God's perfect love for all humanity – not to be feared by disapproval. *"There is no fear in love; but perfect love casteth out fear: because fear hath torment. He that feareth is not made perfect in love"* (I John 4: 18).

~ ~

Darkness – Light

Darkness is the scales over individuals' eyes that limit their inner vision, causing their souls to ache. It is pervasive and casts a shadow over all they do. Darkness is a cesspool of deceit, lies, and fearful situations that lost Christians, who lack common decency, weave to snare and entrap others for their own benefit. The darkness in their minds cannot begin to comprehend what their lives are about. *"And the light shineth in darkness; and the darkness comprehended it not"* (John I: 5).

It is in the darkness that deceit and lies are conceived, and harm is self-inflicted.

"And this is the condemnation, that light is come into the world, and men loved darkness rather than light because their deeds were evil" (John 3: 19).

The dark places in their lives are drawn to the light. It moves slowly but surely to bathe in the light of a comforting and loving God. *"Rejoice not against me, O mine enemy: when I fall, I shall arise; when I sit in darkness, the LORD shall be a light unto me"* (Micah 7: 8).

Christians who have lost their way can change. They can turn toward the light. There is joy in the realization that the light penetrates the darkness. The light that is theirs can never be extinguished. *"The people that walked in darkness have seen a great light: they that dwell in the land of the shadow of death, upon them hath thy light shined"* (Isaiah 9: 2).

These Christians can come through darkness into the light. They may come through the darkness stronger and white as snow. *"Come now, and let us reason together, saith the LORD: though your sins be as scarlet, they shall be as white as snow; though they be red like crimson, they shall be as wool"* (Isaiah I: 18).

If they put on the armor of light, which always reflects the light within them, there would be a mirror reflection of the same. *"The night is far spent, the day is at hand: let us, therefore, cast off the works of darkness, and let us put on the armour of light"* (Romans 13: 12).

From Jesus' darkest moment came His resurrection, and from the depth of the darkest moment may come *their* Easter morning – resurrection. *"The LORD is my light and my salvation; whom shall I fear? The LORD is the strength of my life; of whom shall I be afraid?"* (Psalm 27: 1).

Stop following the bullies of this world. Put off the darkness that surrounds your soul, and come into the light that was yours before entering this plane of opposites. You could once again express the innate nature that dwells within you and treat all human beings with common decency.

4

Who Are You Really?
A Manifestation

Are you a Christian who would continue to endanger your soul? You need to realize who you are. Jesus Christ saved you once. This time around, it is your responsibility.

Energy is what makes the universe and its manifestations possible. In general, vibrational energy produces a wide range of manifestations in the universe, including mental and physical forms. The universe and all its manifestations consist of vibrating energy. Energy has been defined as positive or negative. Vibrating energy is initially just neutral. It is the *use* of it that creates the negative or positive.

There have been in-depth scientific studies involving energy. What is needed to know about energy, as it applies to your state of consciousness, may be realized during a Christ Consciousness Meditation practice (chapter 11). As you practice the Christ Consciousness Meditation, you may become aware of how negative energy may affect your individual consciousness when you are offensive to others. The positive may be experienced as a high energy level when your

Christian common decency is being expressed.

How you express yourself may affect other individuals. You are continually changing the frequency of your state of consciousness as your energy shifts from a slower to a faster speed, from the negative to the positive. You may want to believe you can be cruel to others, and the suffering that you cause does not affect you. Wrong! What you give out, you receive. However, is this all that you are? Or are you more?

You are here on planet Earth, but who are you? Energy, flesh, blood, cells, organs, etc., is that who you are? Think about it. The fact that you can think about it tells you that you must be much more. And you are much more.

Do you understand how *you* are put together? What makes it all work for you to realize that common decency *is* your innate nature? You are not this unchristian image you are portraying as a human being on this earth plane. You are much more.

Consciousness, mind, body, and awareness are how you are put together. The Christ Consciousness Meditation guides you beyond the vibrating energy of your mind-body-consciousness to the silent awareness of your Spiritual Center (chapter 9). It's from here that you may embrace your God-given inherent nature, your Christianity, your DNA.

A basic understanding of how you are put together may allow you to deal with individuals and life's situations with honor and Christian common decency. A review of how you are put together speaks to the effectiveness of realizing who you are.

5

HOW
YOU ARE PUT
TOGETHER
The Three Major Layers

There are three layers of consciousness: physical, mental (psychological), and spiritual. However, there are many levels (frequencies, states) of consciousness that vibrate within the three layers of consciousness. In general, there are many states of consciousness within the three layers of consciousness. However, there are ten major levels (frequencies, states) of consciousness that your individual expression of consciousness may frequently move through, on your inner journey towards the realization of your spirituality.

You are always expressing one of the ten major levels of consciousness, and you are always traveling within them among the many states of consciousness. Therefore, the importance of understanding the ten major levels of consciousness cannot be overstated, as it helps you understand yourself better and communicate with decency across the many individual expressions of consciousness.

TEN MAJOR LEVELS OF CONSCIOUS-NESS:

Level 1: You struggle and suffer in a world of opposites as you seek help in the world of appearances. Attachment to persons and things is the norm.

Level 2: A false sense of a separate self-creates the belief that you must make it on your own.

Level 3: You begin to wonder if there is more than what appears in your life and if there is a better way.

Level 4: There is an inner tugging, a reminder of what you may have had before the world was.

Level 5: Initially, there is resistance to turning within.

Level 6: The resistance begins to fade as you are ready to receive a direct path.

Level 7: As you turn within, an interior cleansing or purification begins.

Level 8: All that is necessary on your inner journey immediately comes forth to meet you on the path and gently guide you during your daily activities.

Level 9: Gradually, with awareness, you access your Spiritual Center and rest. You may begin to gain insights and realizations into Oneness. A personal sense of separation begins to dissolve.

Level 10: Your mind is quick to question that which you call your reality. Doubts arise to question your worthiness. You overcome the doubts. Your awareness deepens as wisdom rises, and a balance emerges between the inner and outer expression of your being.

~~

Now, here is what the problem may be. Since these ten major levels are an individual expression of consciousness, you must keep in mind that although you may be expressing levels 3, 4, or 9, others may be expressing 1, 5, or 7. You may be spending a great deal of time and effort trying to understand and adjust to the various individual expressions of consciousness, including your own. Ignorance of the Oneness of all individual expressions of consciousness contributes to a lack of communication, anxiety, emotional pain, manifested evils, and wars. And yes, a lack of decency.

Ignorance is not a valid excuse under the law. And you cannot plead ignorance when you get to your ultimate destination. We all know what the road to hell is paved with (chapter 12).

6

RETURN
TO
SENDER

No Escape Hatch

Now you may have some idea of why communication can be difficult and why you may lose patience with others. It's not so much that you do not understand one another; you are not always aware of which one of the ten major levels of consciousness you or someone else may be expressing at any given time. It is the same for male-female communication. It's not a "male-female thing." It's a "level-of-individual consciousness thing."

Any of the ten major levels of consciousness may cause a life change that requires an adjustment before you can experience the calm assurance of your ability to communicate proficiently. The Christ Consciousness Meditation (chapters 10 – 11) may reveal the ten major levels of consciousness in a natural progression with as little turmoil as possible. Your interactions with others hinge on who you believe yourself to be. All your beliefs concerning the "self" eventually will manifest. There is no unmanifested consciousness.

You may become more aware of how your daily experiences affect you and those around you. Nothing on this earth is set in concrete. Your individual conscious, mind-personality expression can progress and transform; then, as you change, progression and transformation will manifest in your life, and common decency toward all your fellow human beings will be the order of the day.

Your mistreatment of others in thought, word, or deed affects you more than it would the others you choose to mistreat. Profanity, negativity, and character assassination of others imprint your soul vibration with the same thoughts and words. In reality, the One Consciousness manifests as the many, one of which is yours. Therefore, your conscious-ness is always in a relationship with all indi-vidual expressions of consciousness. You cannot separate who you are from those whom you would harm. It will always "return to sender."

Accepting and respecting your individual expression of consciousness is not always easily done when what manifests or does not manifest is not understood by your state of mind. If your mind's state of consciousness has its way with you, it will hold you in a state of confusion and mental paralysis. The mind state expects to understand not only the seen and known but also the unseen and unknown. It cannot go "there." It twists and turns with what it cannot understand.

Do not underestimate your mind's state of consciousness. It will hold you in *its* place, sap your energy, take away your joy, and involve you in a long-playing drama with the players of your choice. Until you understand the power given to your individual consciousness, you will get caught up in the many doubts, temptations, and trickery that the mind state of consciousness will attempt to impose.

Often, your individual expression of consciousness is not fully appreciated. As a result, you may make demands of it that are not in your best interest. You may tend to forget that your individual expression of consciousness is but one of many on this earth plane. Therefore, common decency is

expected if your inherent nature is to be
expressed.

7

YOUR
INHERENT NATURE
Compassionate Love

Your inherent Christian nature consists of common decency and compassionate love for all. Jesus Christ gave us two great commandments. *"And thou shalt love the Lord thy God with all thy heart, and with all thy soul, and with all thy mind, and with all thy strength: this is the first commandment. And the second is like, namely, this, Thou shalt love thy neighbor as thyself. There is none other commandment greater than these"* (Mark 12: 30-31).

None other is greater than these. If lived by, they render the original ten obsolete. Are you a Christian by label only or a Christian who lives and practices the two great commandments and the teaching of Jesus Christ? There is no room for hate of any kind in the Christ Christian. There are no neighborhoods, only neighbors. To judge all for the misdeeds of a few is a misdeed in itself.

Being baptized and assuming a Christian identity is not necessarily the same as being a practicing Christian or disciple of Jesus Christ. *"For even hereunto were ye called: because Christ also suffered for us, leaving us an example, that ye should follow his steps"* (I Peter 2:21).

A Christian accepts Jesus' invitation to "Come follow me." Jesus Christ is their Lord and teacher. *"And he saith unto them, Follow me, and I will make you fishers of men"* (Matthew 4:19).

Christians' commitment is to awaken to the good news teaching that Jesus Christ shared and for which He gave His life. However, many Christians may be steered in other directions. An arrogant individual and blind obedience to others may prevent wayward Christians from being fully exposed to the teachings of Jesus Christ and a possible close relationship with Jesus.

A true story:

A huge, naked, crazy man stands on a corner and spits on individuals as they pass by. The locals consider him the town's fool and do their best to ignore him. Then, one day a rickshaw driver passes by, and the crazy man spits on him. The rickshaw driver then has his most profitable day ever.

He tells his fellow rickshaw drivers why he believes his good luck is because he was spat on that morning by the crazy fool. Sure enough, the following morning, rickshaw drivers are lining up to be spit upon by the big, crazy fool. The moral of this story: the bigger the fool, the bigger the following.

Are you one who would quickly follow a fool? Don't play the fool. Don't follow one, or be one. To confess Jesus is Lord and then take up with non-Christian practices is like the miner who is easily attracted to fool's gold. It may be shiny and may look like the real thing, but the real thing it is "not."

What is problematic in understanding the "Christ" in Christ-ian? For Christians, Christ is the way. *"And thine ears shall hear a word behind thee, saying This is the way, walk ye in it, when ye turn to the right, and when ye turn to the left"* (Isaiah 30:21).

The Christian journey is a straight and narrow one. It is easy to be seduced by the many broad roads before you. *"Enter ye in at the strait gate: for wide is the gate, and broad is the way that leadeth to destruction, and many there be which go in thereat"* (Matthew 7: 13).

Are you one of the Christians who may, unintentionally, have taken many detours before entering the strait gate and narrow way? Are you one of them? *"Because strait is the gate and narrow is the way, which leadeth unto life, and few there be that find it"* (Matthew 7: 14).

The mind takes a simple truth and weaves it into complex exercises with intellectual jargon. That is what the mind does best. As a Christian of Jesus Christ, follow the teaching of Jesus and keep your focus where it belongs—on the Christ.

You have the greatest master and teacher in Jesus. Do not turn your back on Him. *"In all thy ways acknowledge him, and he shall direct thy paths"* (Proverb 3:6).

Are you a Christian who fears stepping away from the old and moving on to the new? Are you a Christian who can say "yes" when Jesus calls, or do you wear the Christian label and yet journey on other non-Christian paths?

Bouncing about impedes your Christian progress. It is much like picking up two sticks and rubbing them together to start a fire. Your fire will never be lit if you consistently put them down to place your attention elsewhere.

You may be a Christian wandering in the wilderness. You may want to believe you can find your Christian roots in any meditation tradition. On the other hand, you may be satisfied to fill your Christian journey by seeking only a glimpse of what is in your own backyard.

Confusion occurs when you attempt to place your feet in two or more different paths. Which path are you on, a Christian's or a fool's path? Which Christian are you, lost, found/saved, or disciple? *"For many are called, but few are chosen"* (Matthew 22:14).

8

LOST, FOUND/SAVED, DISCIPLE

Which Are You?

Christians fall into three major stages: lost, found/saved, and disciple. They may move about from one stage to another. It is, after all, a Christian journey that consists of many doubts and temptations.

THE THREE CHRISTIAN MAJOR STAGES

3. Christian – Lost

A lost Christian is determined to believe that any of the many different paths include the "strait gate and narrow way." It is why a lost Christian fails to find the strait gate and narrow way. *"Because Strait is the gate, and narrow is the way, which leadeth unto life, and few there be that find it"* (Matthew 7:14).

Because the Christian journey is a strait gate and narrow one, it is easy to be seduced and to get lost on the many broad roads. *"Enter ye in at the strait gate: for wide is the gate, and broad is the way that leadeth to destruction, and many there be which go in thereat"* (Matthew 7:13).

A lost Christian invests time and effort in struggling to hold on to conditioned deceptions. They may find it challenging to give up what has become familiar and to surrender to the unknown. A lost Christian chooses a bunny trail, hopping about from one path to another and strongly resisting the strait gate and narrow way.

A lost Christian avoids the inner journey and wanders from one intellectual path to another, one obscene rally to another. An obnoxious bully may stimulate the mind and cause a psychological high. There may be a constant rise in the mental states of consciousness, and the mind tends to stay where *it* feels good. It is an emotional high, yes, but that is not the Christian way. *"Jesus saith unto him, I am the way, the truth, and the life: no man cometh unto the Father, but by me"* (John 14: 6).

A lost Christian quickly becomes annoyed by any suggested guidance to return to their Christian roots. The intellectual chatter of a bully's world may hold sway. *"... for the letter killeth, but the spirit giveth life"* (II Corinthians 3: 6).

Jesus does not accept the loss of even one of His own. Instead, Jesus perseveres until a lost Christian is safely where they belong. While a lost Christian may seek a foolish bully to follow, Jesus is seeking the lost Christian. *"What man of you, having a hundred sheep, if he loses one of them, doth not leave the ninety and nine in the wilderness, and go after that which is lost until he finds it?"* (Luke 15: 4).

Jesus Christ was more than just a man who once walked the earth. Jesus demonstrated that eternal life is yours. The kingdom He spoke of, and the Father/God that He glorified are yours. *"These things have I written unto you that believe on the name of the of the Son of God; that ye may know that ye have eternal life and that ye may believe on the name of the Son of God"* (I John 5: 13).

Jesus had asked His Father to grant you the glory the Father had given Him. Jesus, who asks this, shares His divine nature with you. Therefore, you cannot separate yourself from that with which you are One. *"And the glory which thou gavest me I have given them; that they may be one, even as we are one"* (John 17: 22).

On this long and challenging Christian journey home, you may have walked many paths, traveled many roads, and climbed many mountains. The journey may seem without end. Why not try Jesus? Why not say "Yes" to Jesus, who never says, "no" to you? Become a *found* Christian. Or, is it more important to deny Jesus than to bend a knee and confess that you require His shepherding? *"And when the chief Shepherd shall appear, ye shall receive a crown of glory that fadeth not away"* (I Peter 5: 4).

2. Christian – Found/Saved

The words "Found/saved" in a Christian setting are much like the word love. They are often used and open to various interpretations *and* misinterpretations. The goal is to enter the presence of the Holy Spirit in the name of Jesus Christ and to know the Father as Jesus knew Him. *"I came forth from the Father, and am come into the world again, I leave the world, and go to the Father"* (John 16: 28).

A Christian's commitment is to awaken to the good news that Jesus shared and for which He was willing to be crucified. Unfortunately, pride may have steered a Christian in other directions. The arrogance of pride may prevent a Christian from being fully exposed to the teachings of Jesus Christ and having a close relationship with Him.

The Christ Consciousness Meditation (chapter 10) may put a found/saved Christian in a position to receive the teachings of Jesus. It may also keep a found/saved Christian's awareness where it belongs — on the Christ. For a found/saved Christian, Jesus Christ is Lord, master, guru, and teacher. There is an acceptance of Jesus' invitation to become a disciple. *"And he saith unto them, Follow me, and I will make you fishers of men"* (Matthew 4: 19).

3. Christian – Disciple

A Christian disciple follows Jesus Christ and His teaching. *"And when he had found him [Saul], he brought him unto Antioch. And it came to pass that they assembled themselves with the church a whole year and taught many people. And the disciples were called Christians first in Antioch"* (Acts 11: 26).

A disciple of Jesus Christ is humble, firm, grounded in uninterrupted truth, and always realizing, *"Ye are of God, little children, and have overcome them: because greater is he that is in you, than he that is in the world"* (I John 4: 4).

There comes a moment in time, on the Christian journey, when an invitation is presented to follow Jesus Christ and *only* Jesus Christ. Jesus does not say to follow Him while you attempt to tag along on a bully's fool path. Following Jesus Christ on a singular path requires your full attention. As it is for Jesus, it is for all who would choose to be a disciple. Discipleship is the acceptance of the spiritual hand of the heavenly Father upon the disciple.

A divided house will fall, and a divided consciousness will struggle to maintain its place. A disciple selects one path and gives it their all. *"And Jesus knew their thoughts, and said unto them, Every kingdom divided against itself is brought to desolation, and every city or house divided against itself shall not stand"* (Matthew 12: 25).

A disciple lives at a time and in a world where many choices are vying for their attention. Jesus' call is one of the many choices, and whether or not *His* call is answered, the disciple has been chosen. *"But ye are a chosen generation, a royal priesthood, a holy nation, a peculiar people; that ye should shew forth the praises of him who hath called you out of darkness into his marvelous light"* (I Peter 2: 9).

Jesus anoints, guides, and directs a disciple's footsteps to the Father's house. There is no greater anointing, no greater discipleship. The confidence and ability to maintain a Christian's walk as a disciple of Jesus Christ are rooted squarely in Christ Consciousness. When the Christ Consciousness Meditation is practiced (chapter 11), the world's bullies may recede, and a disciple's inherent nature may be revealed. Jesus is the way; a disciple needs only to follow. *"And thine ears shall hear a word behind thee, saying This is the way, walk ye in it, when ye turn to the right hand, and when ye turn to the left"* (Isaiah 30: 21).

A disciple is here to wake up. They are servants who do not serve to seek rewards. Nevertheless, the Divine does not let the disciple down. *"That thine alms may be in secret: and thy Father which seeth in secret himself shall reward thee openly"* (Matthew 6: 4).

Accept discipleship in humility and surrender. It is natural for the conscious mind, for a time, to shake at the changing wonders that it must behold. A Christian discipleship manages the mind's doubts and hesitations. *"For with God nothing shall be impossible"* (Luke 1: 37).

A disciple of Jesus Christ is tempted. The appearances of this world do not give up. Temptations come in many different ways. A temptation wants what a disciple has (a realized consciousness) and will appear in any fashion necessary to get it. *"For all that is in the world, the lust of the flesh, and the lust of the eyes, and the pride of life is not of the Father but is of the world"* (I John 2: 16).

~ ~

Did you recognize yourself in any of the Christian stages? There are many questions to ponder and many for you to answer. The Christ Consciousness Meditation may help you to answer, "Which are you— **lost, found/saved, or disciple?"**

Many Christians unintentionally take detours. It is the mind's work to want to take a simple truth and weave it into complex exercises and intellectual jargon. That is what the mind does best.

What greater model could you have than Jesus? What greater model would you want? What greater discipleship is there? *"Herein is my Father glorified, that ye bear much fruit; so shall ye be my disciples"* (John 15: 8).

Lost, found, or disciple, it does not matter. It is easy to get lost, a joy to be found/saved, and an awakening to be a disciple. You are invited to come to a Jesus rally, listen to Him, follow Him, walk with Him, and talk with Him. He awaits the sound of *your* voice. Listen to His (chapter 11). *"That at the name of Jesus every knee should bow, of things in heaven, and things under the earth"* (Philippians 2: 10).

9

The
Spiritual Center
Within You

There is an old tale that goes something like this: after God created humankind, God called one of the angels and asked the angel to hide the one thing God wished to conceal.

"I have finished except for one thing, the mystery of life. Where shall you hide it?" God asked the angel.

"I will hide it in outer space," responded the excited angel.

"No," said God, *"someone one day will easily find it there."*

"All right, I will hide it on the moon. Surely it will not be found there?"

"No, no," said God, *"one day, they will be able to look there also. Mmm,"* thought God. *"I have it! Put it within them. They would never think to look there."*

~~

There is subtle vibrating energy within you (in the chest, between the breasts). It is called the Spiritual Center. Sometimes referred to as the Spiritual Heart Center, the word 'heart' is omitted to avoid confusion with the physical heart.

The Christ Consciousness Meditation addresses a subject rarely discussed by Christians: the Spiritual Center. Christians often ignore the Spiritual Center's availability and access. Why the Spiritual Center? It is the innermost sanctuary of your being. It is the Holy of Holies that is so near, and yet individuals may easily overlook it. It is where the teachings of the Holy Spirit in the name of Jesus Christ emanate.

Within the Spiritual Center, the Holy Spirit, in the name of Jesus, is an active, vibrating energy force. The Holy Spirit is the ultimate teacher. It pours forth and reveals the truth, helping you realize your inherent nature and common decency.

All too often, Christians tend to forget in whose name the Holy Spirit is sent. *"But the Comforter, which is the Holy Ghost, whom the Father will send in my name, he shall teach you all things, and bring all things to your remembrance, whatsoever I have said unto you"* (John 14: 26).

Exactly where is the access to the Spiritual Center? It is neither a mystery nor difficult to find. There is never a time when the Holy Spirit in the name of Jesus is not available. *"Neither pray I for these alone, but for them also which shall believe on me through their word; that they all may be one; as thou Father, art in me, and I in thee, that they also may be one in us: that the world may believe that thou hast sent me"* (John 17: 20-21).

When you practice the Christ Consciousness Meditation (chapter 11), you can access your Spiritual Center and connect with the Holy Spirit in the name of Jesus Christ. Revelations and realizations are born here. The vibrating energy is an invulnerable power. It may dissipate sorrowful remorse, soothe a troubled mind, and restore your relationship with Jesus Christ. It is here that you rest in the shadow of the Almighty. *"He that dwelleth in the secret place of the most High shall abide under the shadow of the Almighty"* (Ps. 91: 1).

A particular Christian practice of the Holy Trinity points to your Spiritual Center. You may be among the many Christians who learned the sign of the cross at an early age but gave it little significance. You honor and express your belief in the Holy Trinity whenever you make the sign of the cross and say, "In the name of the Father (center of forehead), and of the Son (center of chest), and the Holy Spirit. Amen (shoulder to shoulder)."

Making the sign of the cross has *great* significance. When you do so, you point directly to your Spiritual Center. Look in a mirror while making the sign of the cross. Notice that the upper part of your body looks like a cross. You are the cross; you are asked to take up to follow Jesus. *"And he that taketh not his cross, and followeth after me is not worthy of me"* (Matt. 10: 38).

The Spiritual Center is right at your fingertips. Every time you touch the center chest area and say," And of the Son," you are

70

pointing to your Spiritual Center. You have found it. The Christ Consciousness Meditation practice mimics the sign of the cross. It, too, goes directly from your head to your Spiritual Center.

The indwelling light of the Spirit of God beckons you to seek and enter into the Spiritual Center. The darkness and indecency of specific individuals in this world cannot comprehend the light that radiates within you. This light's radiant warmth comforts and holds you in the love of God within your Spiritual Center.

This world knows nothing of the Holy Trinity of your being. It cannot begin to comprehend the things of your divine nature. This world can only marvel in wonderment at a divinity it knows not.

All are invited to become aware of this powerhouse of possibilities. In the powerhouse of your Spiritual Center, the Christ of your being carries you through the shadows of this world's doubts, desires, and temptations. *"For in him we live, and move, and have our being; as certain also of your own poets have said, For we are also his offspring"* (Acts 17: 28).

The Spiritual Center reveals the eternal truth in infinite variety and expression. The purpose of the Christ Consciousness Meditation is to guide you to the awareness of your Spiritual Center area, wherein Christ's presence, common decency, and love prevail. No gift is more magnificent.

Look in the least expected place for the mystery of life — within *your* Spiritual Center. Here is where you may bask with the awareness of your inherent nature and common decency. No code is necessary to become aware of your Spiritual Center; no secret password, introduction, or referral is necessary. Your entrance is assured. It is up to you to become aware of it. Don't let the bullies of this world deprive you of it. It is always within *you.* Go for it!

The Christ Consciousness Meditation is the vessel that carries you across the river into your Spiritual Center. So, get in and take the ride of your life. It is a ride that may take you to the end of the beginning of your life.

10

**The
Christ Consciousness
Meditation**
Revelation

The Christ Consciousness Meditation is a silent, contemplative practice revealed by Jesus Christ. He had insisted, *"Teach them the Christ Consciousness Meditation and be assured; this generation is ready to receive it."* The Christ Consciousness Meditation is offered to help you access your Spiritual Center and establish your relationship with the risen Lord through the power of the Holy Spirit, in the name of Jesus Christ. It is a simple meditation to learn. It acknowledges and builds upon all previous contemplative teaching, tradition, and biblical reference.

What makes the Christ Consciousness Meditation the pearl of great price, the Holy Grail of silent meditations? It is a revelation – the strait gate and narrow way to the Holy Spirit in the name of Jesus Christ. The Christ

75

Consciousness Meditation is a unique contribution to the inner journey. It is the direct path to your inner life with Jesus Christ and your inherent nature, common decency.

The Christ Consciousness Meditation's simplicity is its difficulty and strength. Its most significant difficulty is that it is an easy practice. You will encounter no complicated instructions, rigid rules, or demanding postures. Individuals are accustomed to meditations that require a measure of difficulty. As a result, easy becomes difficult. However, it is also its strength; to be so easy and yet so profound in its ability to reveal truth. It can only leave you in awe!

All meditations have their value, but they differ from one another. The Christ Consciousness Meditation cuts to the chase. It allows nothing to stand between you and the spirituality of your God, through the power of the Holy Spirit, in the name of Jesus Christ.

You may be firmly established in truth. Rooted and grounded in love, your silent meditation and life are built upon hallowed ground. *"That Christ may dwell in your hearts by faith; that ye, being rooted and grounded in love, May be able to comprehend with all saints what is the breadth, and length, and height; And to know the love of Christ, which passeth knowledge, that ye might be filled with all the fullness of God"* (Eph. 3: 17-19).

The Christ Consciousness Meditation does not separate your inner practice from your outer practical living. On the contrary, when you practice it with a determined purpose, the fruits of love, joy, peace, goodness, kindness, meekness, gentleness, patience, and common decency may express themselves naturally in your daily life. As individual expressions of divine love, these fruits testify to God's purifying, loving, and healing presence.

Once you have the courage to turn within and live in quiet silence, you may realize it is your nature—the inner and the outer merge in a calm, peaceful environment. The silence allows the awareness of the Christ to express its presence naturally. Unfortunately, living with constant background noise and the chatter of your home environment obscures the quiet silence.

Making a change from your regular routine can be a challenge. You have been conditioned "to do" and sometimes "overdo" to get what you want. You push, shove, and drive yourself to the brink to get what it is you believe you want. It is always getting and holding on. Effort, effort, all is an effort.

Now you are instructed to do the opposite of what you have been taught: no pushing, no shoving, no holding on, and no driving yourself anywhere. The most significant effort is to show up, practice the Christ Consciousness Meditation one minute twice daily, and be patient. Your journey is unique to you.

The mind takes you on an outer journey where bullies often govern the attraction of appearances and false concepts. The Christ Consciousness Meditation takes you on an inner journey to the aware spirituality of your being. Jesus went beyond the traditions and teachings of His day. Jesus revealed through His example and teaching that you, too, can go beyond the traditions of your day. Jesus never condemned traditional teachings. He fulfilled the law while revealing life eternal. His is a kingdom not of this world. The Christ Consciousness Meditation may slowly, carefully, and lovingly restore the remembrance of that kingdom.

The God that is known by faith dwells within you always. The Christ Consciousness Meditation is for those interested in responding to God without mental or verbal words in solitude, simplicity, and silence. Jesus guides you through His Holy Spirit to God's spirituality. *"Jesus saith unto him, I am the way, the truth, and the life: no man cometh unto the Father, but by me"* (John 14: 6).

The bullies of this world fear what they do not understand or cannot destroy. This world believed it could destroy and put to death Jesus' teaching of salvation and freedom. It could not. It did not.

The following comments are from participants in Christ Consciousness Meditation. They tell how the Christ Consciousness

Meditation worked for them. It may also work for you.

Comments:

- "The presence of my Lord is realized."

- "I sleep better, and my health has improved."

- "My children tell me I'm easier to get along with."

- "I am more balanced and stable in everything I do."

- "I am more flexible when things don't go my way."

- "I am less prone to anger and to harbor resentments."

- "It is a life-changing event. The silence is profound."

- "I experience more joy in my life and more self-acceptance."

- "I am happier, and my friends say, 'You're nicer to be around.'"

- "I have more clarity and discernment in my business decisions."

- "My life seems to unfold with less stress, clarity, and ease."

- "My emotional responses to life's ups and downs are more appropriate and less exaggerated."

~~

In coming home to the spirituality of their being at the deepest level, the participants report an ability to remember what their lives are all about. By faithfully practicing the Christ Consciousness Meditation, folks reported returning to their daily activities with renewed energy and a refreshed sense of purpose. The comment most often made was, "It changed my life." Such reports incentivize you to practice the Christ Consciousness Meditation and reap its benefits.

The Christ Consciousness Meditation fulfills Jesus' invitation to "come and find rest for your souls." With Jesus as a model, scriptures as a reference, tradition as custodian, sacraments as a celebration, and selfless service as a mission, the Christ Consciousness Meditation draws its source, sustenance, and direction.

Telling you a Spiritual Center exists is not enough. Telling you about the Christ Consciousness Meditation is not enough. Telling you to turn within is not enough. Telling you where to turn within is not enough. Telling you about participants' comments is not enough. You *must* know *how to* turn within to access your Spiritual Center. The Christ Consciousness Meditation practice *is* the *"how to."*

11

The
Practice
Three Easy Steps

As a follower of Jesus Christ, you may take the "strait gate and narrow way" to accepting Jesus Christ as your guide and master. The Christ Consciousness Meditation practice may carefully respond to Jesus' invitation to "follow me." It may painstakingly lead you on a spiritual journey to your all-inclusive God in spirit and truth presence.

The Christ Consciousness Meditation practice articulates a simplification. It does not require any aids because, in your spirituality, *you are* the sacred w*ord* that existed in the beginning. *"In the beginning was the Word, and the Word was with God, and the Word was God. The same was in the beginning with God. All things were made by him, and without him was not anything made that was made"* (John 1: 1-3).

The Practice:

1. Sit comfortably, close your eyes, deeply inhale, and slowly exhale. Then, relaxing your entire body, continue to breathe normally.

2. Consciously become aware of your Spiritual Center *area* (center of the chest, between the breasts) and rest with the awareness of the *area*.

3. When thoughts or sensations arise, do not dialogue, converse, engage, or respond. Again, with awareness, become aware of your Spiritual Center *area* and rest there.

Is that not easy? There is no need to complicate The Christ Consciousness Meditation practice. Easy *does* work. The practice takes you directly to your Spiritual Center. First, however, *you* must do the practice.

Hearing, touching, seeing, tasting, and smelling – are impressions received through the physical body organs of perception. These sense impressions and thinking may draw your immediate attention. Again, become aware of your Spiritual Center area and rest with awareness of the *area*. You are not seeking to feel anything. You are just resting with the awareness of your Spiritual Center *area*.

Practice the silent Christ Consciousness Meditation at any time before and at least two hours after a meal (the changing energy vibration will interfere with the digestion process). Begin the meditation for one minute and allow it to extend naturally over time. There is no prescribed length of time required. One minute is an eternity with the awareness of your spirituality.

At the end of a meditation period, open your eyes, move your hands, and move your feet. Before returning to your normal activities, take a moment to become consciously aware of your mental and physical senses as they arise. Remember, you are not trying to make anything happen. You are not seeking to *feel* anything. The mind feels. You are resting with awareness of your Spiritual Center *area* beyond the mind and body states of consciousness.

Be consistent and practice the Christ Consciousness Meditation twice-a-day. When sitting on a chair, you may wish to sit on a chair with arms for support. Sitting on a cushion on the floor and using a prayer shawl are options

An Old Habit

You may already have formed the habit of practicing a different meditation. An established habit is not always easy to discontinue, especially if it is one of long-standing. A habit is an act of interest often repeated. Replacing one habitual meditation practice with another need not be difficult.

Do not get upset if a previous meditation practice rises to compete with your new practice. To struggle only reinforces the old habit. With loving-kindness, allow the old established meditation practice to rise and treat it as you would any other thought. Do not dialogue; again, with awareness, become aware of your Spiritual Center area and rest on your Spiritual Center. Gradually, the old practice will no longer rise.

It is not wise or useful to judge or evaluate your practice based on experiences. The fruit of the meditation may be realized daily, as the Holy Spirit in the name of Jesus Christ insinuates itself spontaneously. *"But the fruit of the Spirit is love, joy, peace, long-suffering, gentleness, goodness, faith, meekness, temperance: against such there is no law"* (Galatians 5: 22-23).

The Christ Consciousness Meditation practice facilitates your participation in the divine word, which you are. Without extraneous dialogue, stringent guidelines, or complicated definitions, the Christ Consciousness Meditation practice bypasses potential distractions that the mind loves to create. The practice may easily and effortlessly open your Spiritual Center directly to the awareness of the Divine Presence. Through direct invitation and guidance of the Holy Spirit in the name of Jesus Christ you may be led to the realization and awareness of the risen Lord.

Jesus is with you every step of the way. He is with you through your fears, ups, and downs. Be assured; your spiritual journey *is* His priority. Jesus does not give one moment and take away the next. No, Jesus does not play like that. *"LORD, thou hast been our dwelling place in all generations"* (Ps. (90: 1).

Jesus is not with you until death do you part, but for life eternal because as Jesus is in the Father, you are in Jesus, and Jesus is in you. *"At that day ye shall know that I am in my Father, and ye in me, and I in you"* (John 14: 20).

You may realize that your inner and outer life share much in common. In reality, all life is a spiritual activity. Whether washing dishes, scrubbing floors, or sitting in silent meditation, you may come to do all things with conscious awareness and with common decency. Your inner guidance is seamless. You may become as aware of God's abiding presence in your practical living as you are during your silent meditation practice.

Flexibility

Be flexible. Flexibility gives you the freedom to adjust to new routines. An active lifestyle requires flexibility: any change to a routine can create resistance. All too often, you may be attached to a particular schedule, time, or place. You may want everything to be the same day after day. In most situations, this might seem ideal.

Flexibility is a nurturing skill that helps you to be kinder to yourself and others. Go with what you have, wherever you are. If you find that fitting in daily second practice is difficult – you can't find the time because of work, errands, children, and many other things on your agenda that interfere – this is understandable.

Here's a suggestion: you go to the bathroom sometime during your busy day, right? Stay on the John for an extra minute. It's that easy. Your friend, John, can be beneficial. In fact, John may become your *best* friend!

12

Accept, Allow, and Respect

What the Road to Hell Is Paved With

The Christ Consciousness Meditation practice is necessary because words won't get the job done, and good intentions never lift a finger. Besides, we all know what the road to hell is paved with. So, pay close attention to this story. It could involve you.

A pompous, self-righteous individual dies. When he arrives "up there," he notices how well everyone gets along. He approaches Saint Peter, who is in his splendor of brilliance.

Glancing at the man and eager to know why he is there, Saint Peter asks, *"What is it you want?"*

Belligerently, the man responds, *"I want to stay here!"*

Amazed, Saint Peter asks, *"Oh? Why is that?"*

In exhilaration, the man replies, *"It's wonderful here. Everyone seems to get along. They are so kind, thoughtful."*

"Yes," Saint Peter says. *"We are appreciative of each individual. The rule of heaven is common decency from all to all. Were you kind and decent with others while you were on earth?"*

Waving off Saint Peter's implication with an impersonal dismissal, the man says,

"Well, it's like this: I had myself to think about. You know how that is. There was never enough time to consider others, and by the time I got to the top of my game, I was here. But be assured, I planned on improving my relationships. I always had good intentions."

Softly smiling, Saint Peter replies, *"Ah! You are looking for the other place. The road to it is paved with good intentions."*

~~

When you get upset and insist that you know better, it's your ego gone amiss. All that you do for others, you are doing for yourself. An act of common decency reflects *your* Divine nature. There is never any time when you are doing anyone a favor. The favor is for you.

When you are agitated by others' behavior, stop, look to yourself, and ask, "Why does this upset me? What is going on with *me*?"

Like a washing machine that agitates dirty clothes until they come clean, your inner guidance agitates until your vibrating energy is clean. Accept, allow, and respect others' choices and decisions. The Christ Consciousness Meditation is about working with *your* emotions, *responses, doubts, and* temptations.

The universe exists within consciousness. Therefore, all that exists in the universe exists within consciousness. Therefore, work must begin within you to have a healthy, contented life.

Your outer actions reflect your inner individual moral sense of your Christian common decency. However, to maintain a healthy balance in your outer world, there must first be a healthy balance within your consciousness and vibrating energy. That's the work of the Christ Consciousness Meditation practice.

Your vibrating energy field affects how you treat yourself, others, and everything around you. The Christ Consciousness Meditation's direct path of awareness helps you understand the power within your Spiritual Center, enabling you to create a healthy balance. Your outer life conforms to the inner, not the other way around. You have an inner power that pierces the illusion of an inner-outer separation. It's not separation. It's a reflection.

Time

The best time to be aware of the importance of the Christ Consciousness Meditation in your life is *now.* Playing the waiting game is a disastrous stall—waiting cuts into creativity and ingenuity, prolonging your pain and suffering. Waiting for the right moment to begin the Christ Consciousness Meditation practice, or waiting for another to act first, is a waste of time.

Part of realizing your Christian common decency is to accept, allow, and respect others' rights to make choices and decisions for themselves so that you can get on with the work that *begins with you.* There are benefits to accepting, allowing, and respecting yourself and others. These benefits allow you to move beyond conflicts of interest.

ACCEPT

- Acceptance of others frees you from judging.

- To accept any given moment reveals the present.

- When you accept others, you are accepting yourself, which is an expression of self-love.

ALLOW

- You will lose fewer friends if you are patient with those who disagree.

- Choosing not to criticize those with different views will deepen your conscious awareness.

- Allowing others to be where they are may reduce expectations, stress, and struggles.

RESPECT

- Respect for yourself and others is an expression of Christian common decency that may bring about compromise.

- When you respect the beliefs of others, you suffer less from emotional turmoil.

- Giving others the respect you believe you deserve contributes to a positive state of mind.

~~

A conflict of interest is at its greatest intensity when you insist on holding on to the familiar while the new overshadows it. A conflict of interest dissolves when you can let go of the familiar. So let go of being a bully and meanness, and allow your Christian common decency to express itself.

Conclusion

Where Are All The Christians?

"How long shall they utter and speak hard things? And all the workers of iniquity boast themselves?" (Ps. 94:4).

Our great nation needs brave, pure souls to step forward and be willing to pay the price to stop the savaging of a tarnished Nation. Unfortunately, the bullies, the lack of leadership, and the Evangelicals willing to tarnish their souls for *their* religious beliefs are all complicit. These are disguised Christians. Their true colors are not an example that Jesus Christ set. Jesus would not and did not go along to get along.

Often in my lifetime, I have heard, "How did Hitler come to power? How was he able to rule over so many? Well, now we know. Destroying trust in our institutions and the free press, and coercing those who pretend to serve, is how it is done. Is there still hope for a Nation on life support? I pray there is. But it will take all Christians to realize they are paying a greater price than what they are being given in return for allowing the Nation to suffer.

Yes, they could have a pinch of consciousness and remember they are the Christians we are looking for and counting on, but will they? The judgment placed on their heads is not for us to set, but to put a stop to the obvious; it is our responsibility. Where are all the Christians? Where have they gone?

Author / Translator

Carla R. Mancari is an author, translator, life guide, and teacher. She seeks to improve the self-confidence and self-esteem of individuals from all walks of life so that they can meet life's challenges. For more than 45 years, she has guided individuals in understanding life's spiritual principles, activities, and rising emotions in their private and daily lives.

Carla is the recipient of the Christ Consciousness Meditation and the Minute Meditation. Although she had never attended high school and was labeled a retarded child, she attained two University degrees: a B.A. from the University of South Carolina in Columbia, South Carolina, and an MEd from South Carolina State University in Orangeburg, South Carolina. Carla studied at Brigham Young University and attended the School of the Americas in Switzerland.

Carla led a class action lawsuit in the United States Supreme Court to protect minorities' rights (Morton v. Mancari, 1973) and was a certified psychologist. She served in the United States Air Force. Traveling worldwide for many years, Carla studied with Christian, Hindu, and Buddhist masters. She was a guest on the Larry King Radio Show and a guest lecturer at various colleges, professional groups, book clubs, and at book signings.

Carla gained national recognition when featured in *Good Housekeeping*, "The Education of Carla Mancari, 1969." It chronicled her life in 1967-68 when she was the first white woman to receive a Master's degree from the all-Black South Carolina State College in Orangeburg, South Carolina. She is the author of many books. Carla's greatest joy is helping individuals realize their self-worth, unique gifts/talents, and full potential, and wake up to their spiritual reality.

Books

Mancari, Carla R., *The Lessons: How to Understand Spiritual Principles, Spiritual Activities and Rising Emotions, A Comprehensive Collection.* Celestial Literary Group, 2026.

- - - *Christ Consciousness Meditation Practice: Pocket Size.* Celestial Literary Group, 2026.

- - - *Loneliness.* Celestial Literary Group, 2026.

- - - *Racism, Antisemitism+: A Disease of the Mind.* Celestial Literary Group, 2026.

- - - *The Christ Consciousness Meditation Teaching Guide.* Celestial Literary Group, 2026.

- - - *Metaphysical Questions with Answers from the Christ Consciousness.* Celestial Literary Group, 2026.

- - - *When Jesus Is the Guru: A Wayward Christian's Spiritual Walk.* Celestial Literary Group, 2010.

- - - *Eco-You: A Power of One, Improve Your Health, Improve Your Life.* Celestial Literary Group, 2019.

- - - *Walking on the Grass: A White Woman In A Black World.* Celestial Literary Group, 2016.

- - - *Abortion and The Bible: The Abortion Dilemma: A Scriptural Response, A Woman's Spirituality.* Celestial Literary Group, 2017.

- - - *Racism: The Pain of Invisibility.* Celestial Literary Group, 2017.

- - - *The Rising Emotions: Understanding and Mastering Them.* Celestial Literary Group, 2017.

- - - *The Mystical Path: The Serious Student.* Celestial Literary Group, 2017.

- - - *Spiritual Principles: Understanding, Realizing, and Living Them.* Celestial Literary Group, 2018.

- - - *Climate Change: Consciousness Change.* Celestial Literary Group, 2017.

- - - *Words: Locks On The Door or Keys To The Kingdom.* Celestial Literary Group, 2018.

- - - *Aging: Physical to the Mystical.* Celestial Literary Group, 2018.

- - - *Divine Love: Your Nature.* Celestial Literary Group, 2018.

- - - *The Lazarus Rising: The Kundalini – A Rising Dormant Energy.* Celestial Literary Group, 2018.

- - - *Depression: Hopelessness – A Disconnection.* Celestial Literary Group, 2018.

- - - *Jesus Christ: Teacher.* Celestial Literary Group, 2018.

- - - *The Mystical Surrender: Giving In.* Celestial Literary Group, 2018.

- - - *Death Ain't Dead: Empty Graves.* Celestial Literary Group, 2018.

- - - *Common Decency: Your DNA.* Celestial Literary Group, 2018.

- - - *Christians?: Common Decency.* Celestial Literary Group, 2018.

- - - *Beyond Buddhism: Meditations.* Celestial Literary Group, 2018.

- - - *Exit: Get Ready, Set, Go.* Celestial Literary Group, 2018.

- - - *Meditation: Good For You.* Celestial Literary Group, 2018.

- - - *How To Love "You": Begins with You.* Celestial Literary Group, 2018.

- - - *Consciousness: Yours.* Celestial Literary Group, 2018.

- - - *Suicide: Understanding It.* Celestial Literary Group, 2018.

- - - *Detachment: Realizations.* Celestial Literary Group, 2018.

- - - *Detachment: Christian.* Celestial Literary Group, 2018.

- - - *Sexual Abuse By The Church – Its Root, Coerced Celibacy.* Celestial Literary Group, 2018.

- - - *Guns and Guts: The Courage To Act.* Celestial Literary Group, 2018.

- - - *Jesus, The Way: A Mystical Understanding.* Celestial Literary Group, 2019.

- - - *Motivation: Self-Motivated.* Celestial Literary Group, 2019.

- - - *Totally Free: Is Killing Me.* Celestial Literary, Group, 2018.

- - - *A 30-Second Meditation For Teenagers.* Celestial Literary Group, 2018.

- - - *A 30-Second Meditation For Seniors.* Celestial Literary Group, 2017.

- - - *The Five Faces Of Love.* Celestial Literary Group, 2019.

- - - *Angel In The House.* Celestial Literary Group, 2019 (A Children's Book).

- - - *Put It In The Bible: Prayerful Requests.* Celestial Literary Group, 2019.

- - - *Hate: A Dark Emotion.* Celestial Literary Group, 2019.

- - - *Greed: It's Addictive.* Celestial Literary Group, 2019.

- - - *On Being Young: Choices.* Celestial Literary Group, 2019.

- - - *Gratitude: Expressed, Sincere.* Celestial Literary Group, 2019.

- - - *Humor: A Necessity.* Celestial Literary Group, 2019.

- - - *A Christian: Are You One?* Celestial Literary Group, 2019.

- - - *Habit: How To Switch Meditation Practices.* Celestial Literary Group, 2019.

- - - *Impeachment: Living On The Dark Side.* Celestial Literary Group, 2019.

- - - *The Jesus I Know.* Celestial Literary Group, 2019.

- - - *Grace: Spirit And Truth.* Celestial Literary Group, 2019.

- - - *Temptation.* Celestial Literary Group, 2019.

- - - *The Christian Journey: Teacher Student Relationship.* Celestial Literary Group, 2019.

- - - *The Beloved: Who Is The Beloved?* Celestial Literary Group, 2019.

- - - *What Now, Lord? Enlightenment.* Celestial Literary Group, 2019.

- - - *What If I Were Gay?* Celestial Literary Group, 2019.

- - - *Mother Mary: Mother of Jesus.* Celestial Literary Group, 2019.

- - - *I Remember America.* Celestial Literary Group, 2019.

- - - *The Overcoming: Jesus.* Celestial Literary Group, 2019.

- - - *When Faith Is Not Enough.* Celestial Literary Group, 2019.

- - - *The Plane of Opposites: The Work.* Celestial Literary Group, 2020.

- - - *Crisis.* Celestial Literary Group, 2020.

- - - *Grief: Gut-Wrenching Emotion.* Celestial Literary Group, 2020.

- - - *God.* Celestial Literary Group, 2020.

- - - *Regrets: Do You Have Any?* Celestial Literary Group, 2020.

- - - *1968, 1968,1968: The Mind of A Racist.* Celestial Literary Group, 2020.

- - - *Satan.* Celestial Literary Group, 2020.

- - - *Practice Practice: Meditation.* Celestial Literary Group, 2021.

- - - *Christians Without Jesus: Prodigal Son's Journey.* Celestial Literary Group, 2021.

- - - *From Here To There.* Celestial Literary Group, 2021.

- - - *An Awakening Path: Christian Spiritual Principles.* Celestial Literary Group, 2021.

- - - *Holy Scriptures: Uplifting, Inspiring and Comforting.* Celestial Literary Group, 2021.

- - - *Male Female: The Split Soul.* Celestial Literary Group, 2021.

- - - *The Inner Message: Theological Mystical State.* Celestial Literary Group, 2021.

- - - *A Guide To Understanding Mind's Contents And Realizations.* Celestial Literary Group, 2021.

- - - *A Sister's Laughter: Oh! How I Miss It* Celestial Literary Group, 2021.

- - - *Churches: Are They Necessary?* Celestial Literary Group, 2021.

- - - *Metaphysical: Stories and Poems.* Celestial Literary Group, 2021.

- - - *Jesus, Jesus, Jesus.* Celestial Literary Group, 2021.

- - - *The Disciple and The Mystical Guide.* Celestial Literary Group, 2021.

- - - *The Holy Trinity: 1+1+1=1, No Mystery.* Celestial Literary Group, 2021.

- - - *Fear of Jesus: Why?.* Celestial Literary Group, 2021.

- - - *Symbols and Rituals: Christian.* Celestial Literary Group, 2021.

- - - *Christian Minute Meditation.* Celestial Literary Group, 2021.

- - - *Sin!.* Celestial Literary Group, 2021.

- - - *Compassion.* Celestial Literary Group, 2021.

- - - *Silence.* Celestial Literary Group, 2021.

- - - *The Spiritual Zone.* Celestial Literary Group, 2022.

- - - *The Bible Scriptures: Mystical Understanding.* Celestial Literary Group, 2022.

- - - *Lead Us Not Into Temptation: The Lord's Prayer.* Celestial Literary Group, 2022.

- - - *Let's Talk About Jesus, Or Not.* Celestial Literary Group, 2022.

- - - *For The Love of Jesus: Come Back To Your Church.* Celestial Literary Group, 2022.

- - - *Abortion, When Life Does Not Begin! Exodus 21:22-25.* Celestial Literary Group, 2022.

- - - *Morton vs. Mancari: A Plaintiff's Response: How An Average Joe (woman) Landed In The US Supreme Court.* Celestial Literary Group, 2022.

- - - *Christian Spiritual Exercises: The Inner Journey.* Celestial Literary Group, 2023.

- - - *The Kingdom Of God – A Gift.* Celestial Literary Group, 2023.

- - - *An Expression of Love.* Celestial Literary Group, 2023.

- - - *Choices and Decisions On a Spiritual Journey.* Celestial Literary Group, 2024.

- - - *Love Your Enemies: How Can You Do That?.* Celestial Literary Group, 2024.

- - - *Outer Space and Inner Space Travel.* Celestial Literary Group, 2024.

- - - *God – Love: Poets Write About It.* Celestial Literary Group, 2024.

- - - *The Still Small Voice, You Can Hear It.* Celestial Literary Group, 2024.

- - - *The Resurrection: Rising Beyond Body Consciousness.* Celestial Literary Group, 2024.

- - - *Sexual Spiritual Intercourse: Oneness.* Celestial Literary Group, 2024.

- - - *Child Of God: In Spirit and Truth.* Celestial Literary Group, 2024.

- - - *"My Child," Blessed Mother Mary's.* Celestial Literary Group, 2024.

- - - *Strait Gate and Narrow Way: "Few There Be That Find It".* Celestial Literary Group, 2024.

- - - *Strait Gate and Narrow Way: "Few There Be That Find It", Pocket Size.* Celestial Literary Group, 2024.

- - - *The End Of The Beginning, Our Spiritual Journey.* Celestial Literary Group, 2024.

- - - *A Cat Story.* Celestial Literary Group, 2025.

Mancari, Carla. R. *and* Carpenter, Mary B. *Scriptural Reference For - The Lessons, A*

Comprehensive Collection. Celestial Literary Group, 2026.

- - -*The Minute Meditation, Book 1: It Is Profound!* Celestial Literary Group, 2022.

- - -*The Minute Meditation, Book 2: Workbook, It Is Profound!*. The Celestial Literary Group, 2022.

- - - *The Minute Meditation, It Is Profound! Book 3: The Essentials*. Celestial Literary Group, 2022.

- - - *The Minute Meditation, It Is Profound! Book 4: A Diet For The Soul*. Celestial Literary Group, 2022.

- - - *The Minute Meditation, It Is Profound! Book 5: The Three of You, You Are Never Alone*. Celestial Literary Group, 2022.

- - - *The Minute Meditation, It Is Profound! Book 6: Pocket Size*. Celestial Literary Group, 2022.

- - - *The Minute Meditation, It Is Profound! Book 7 – Teaching Guide*. Celestial Literary Group, 2022.

- - - *The Minute Meditation, It Is Profound! Book 8 – The 4th Chakra*. Celestial Literary Group, 2026.

- - - *Spirituality: Yours.* Celestial Literary Group, 2021.

- - - *Dreams: States of Consciousness.* Celestial Literary Group, 2021.

- - - *A Christian Service With A Silent Christian Meditation.* Celestial Literary Group, 2024.

Casey-Martus, Sandra, and Mancari, Carla R. *The Lessons: How to Understand Spiritual Principles, Spiritual Activities, and Rising Emotions, Lessons with Stories Along a Spiritual Journey.* Celestial Literary Group, 2026.

NOTES

www.ingramcontent.com/pod-product-compliance
Lightning Source LLC
Chambersburg PA
CBHW012258240726
48656CB00007B/2430